EVERYDAY ECONOMICS
BORROWING

Tatiana Tomljanovic

Weigl Publishers Inc.

Published by Weigl Publishers Inc.
350 5th Avenue, Suite 3304, PMB 6G
New York, NY 10118-0069

Website: www.weigl.com

Library of Congress Cataloging-in-Publication Data available upon request.
Fax 1-866-44-WEIGL for the attention of the Publishing Records department.

ISBN 978-1-60596-645-8 (hard cover)
ISBN 978-1-60596-646-5 (soft cover)

Printed in China
1 2 3 4 5 6 7 8 9 0 13 12 11 10 09

Every reasonable effort has been made to trace ownership and to obtain permission to reprint
copyright material. The publishers would be pleased to have any errors or omissions brought
to their attention so that they may be corrected in subsequent printings.

Weigl acknowledges Getty Images as its primary image supplier for this title.

smart investing
@ your library

A partnership between American Library Association
and FINRA Investor Education Foundation

ALA American Library Association

FINRA Investor Education FOUNDATION

FINRA is proud to support the American Library Association

Project Coordinator **Heather C. Hudak** | Designer **Terry Paulhus** | Layout **Kenzie Browne**

CONTENTS

BORROWING VOCABULARY

ECONOMY the production, distribution, and consumption of goods and services
FEE money paid for a service
INTEREST money paid at a regular rate for the use of a loan

What Is Borrowing?

Borrowing is when a person takes something from another person with the intention of returning it at a later date.

Borrowing is an important part of the **economy**. Whenever a person buys something, such as a book or a bag of apples, they are taking part in the economy. Selling something, such as lemonade at a lemonade stand, is also taking part in the economy. Collecting a **fee** for performing a service, such as mowing a neighbor's lawn, is another way to take part in the economy.

The exchange of money for goods and services is the base of economic activity. Sometimes, people do not have enough money to buy certain goods and services. If they want a product or a service immediately, they

People who want to buy a boat or sail around the world on vacation may need to borrow money to pay for these expenses.

may try to borrow money to pay for it rather than wait until they have enough money saved. The key to borrowing money is to understand that, at some point, the money must be repaid to the lender.

Usually, lenders are paid a fee for the use of their money. This fee, called **interest**, is a percentage of the amount borrowed multiplied by the amount of time it takes to pay back the borrowed money.

A common reason people borrow money is so that they can buy a new home.

When Did Borrowing Begin?

People have been borrowing from others for thousands of years, even before money was first used. People would **barter** for goods and services. Sometimes, a person would borrow an item, such as a cow. This would be returned with interest, in the form of two cows, at a later date.

100,000 years ago Shell jewelry, beads, and other rare items are traded for basic items, such as food.

3000 BC **Mesopotamians** use coins called shekels as **currency**. A shekel was a specific mass of barley that was equal to a certain value of silver, bronze, or copper.

Around 1780 BC The Code of Hammurabi is created in Babylon. The code, along with earlier laws, formalizes

100,000 years ago   Around 1780 BC   330 BC

the role of money in cities. The laws set amounts of interest to be paid on **debts** and fines for breaking the law.

330 BC Egyptian farmers store grain in royal warehouses for safekeeping. Farmers are given warehouse receipts as a form of money.

325 AD The First Council of Nicæa, an assembly representing Christian churches, forbids **usury**.

800 Paper money is used in China during the Tang Dynasty.

1545 King Henry VIII of England gives English citizens permission to charge interest on loans.

1791 The First Bank of the United States opens. The United States establishes a banking system and its own currency.

1920 The United States has 30,000 banks. This is more than all of the banks in the rest of the world.

1950 The first credit card is invented by Frank McNamara. It is named the Diners Club credit card. A seven percent fee is charged for each transaction using the card, as well as a $3 annual fee.

2005 Walter Cavanagh holds the Guinness Book of World Records title of "Mr. Plastic Fantastic" for having the most credit cards of anyone in the world, with 1,497.

800   1950   2005

Money Through the Ages

Bartering was very common in ancient times. For example, farmers who grew wheat often had more grain than they needed. They would trade some of their grain for a cow so they would have fresh milk to drink. However, farmers needed milk year round, but they only harvested their grain in the autumn. They had no wheat to trade for the rest of the year. This created a need for another form of payment, such as coins.

Metal was made into coins that could be traded for goods and services. Until modern times, the worth of a coin was measured by the weight of the metal from which it was made. This is known as commodity money. For example, a British pound was once worth

For centuries, people having been trading coins and other valuable items in exchange for goods and services.

a pound of sterling silver. Eventually, coins were marked with a value. This value is often not equal to the weight of the coin.

Commodity money developed into representative money. Banks would give people who deposited gold and silver coins in their bank a paper receipt. The receipt could be exchanged at a later date for the same amount of gold and silver that was originally deposited. People began trading receipts as money because everyone knew they were "as good as gold."

Today, bills and coins are not backed by another commodity, such as gold. This is called fiat money. Fiat money is given value by the government. Most governments, including the United States, use fiat money.

A bank lends out more money than it has on site. If everyone who deposited money into a bank wanted their fiat money back at the exact same time, the bank would not be able to pay everyone.

BORROWING VOCABULARY

GLOBAL RECESSION worldwide economic slowdown
INSURED protected against damage or loss
STABLE stays the same
RESTRICTIONS limitations or rules on who can borrow money

Where Do People Borrow Money?

It is common for people to borrow money from a parent, close relative, or a friend. Money borrowed from these people sometimes is called "love money."

One of the most common places to borrow money from is a bank. Banks are places where people store their money in accounts. When people put money in a bank, they know their funds are safe. Banks are **insured** against theft and other events, such as fire. However, banks do not keep all of this money on site. They lend the money that people deposit to other people and companies.

Loans and mortgages are two common ways to borrow from a bank. Banks lend money to people in the form of a mortgage or loan for a certain period of time. During this time, the money is paid back in one or more payments each month. Banks charge a fee for borrowing money. This fee is another form of interest. It is a percentage of the amount borrowed.

Credit unions, trust companies, and mortgage loan companies are other types of financial institutions that loan money.

Large loans with few **restrictions** can be dangerous. From 2000 to 2008, U.S. mortgage loan companies loaned money with very high interest rates to people who could not afford to pay the loans back. Many people lost their homes. This problem, along with other factors, led to a **global recession**. Responsible borrowing and lending is important to a **stable** economy.

Money Lenders

These are a few common types of money lenders.

Credit Unions

Credit unions are owned and controlled by their members. People who have accounts with a credit union also own part of the credit union. Credit unions tend to be smaller than banks.

Mortgage Originators

Mortgage originators help people secure funds for the specific purpose of buying a home or office. Mortgage brokers and bankers are orginators. Brokers do not have money to lend. Instead, they help the borrower find a financial institution to loan them the money. Mortgage bankers use their own money to lend borrowers. Often, they sell the mortgage to an investor or financial institution. Mortgage originators earn fees for setting up the loan. Mortgage loan companies have fewer restrictions on borrowing money than banks. It is easier to get approved for a loan from a mortgage loan company than from a bank.

Trust Companies

Trust companies are hired to manage money, keep records, and pay bills. They are usually owned by an independent company, bank, or law firm.

BORROWING VOCABULARY

COLLATERAL valuable items a person owns and can promise to give to the money lender if he or she is unable to repay debts

Types of Loans

There are two basic types of loans. Every type of loan is either a form of secured borrowing or unsecured borrowing.

Unsecured borrowing

Unsecured borrowing happens when the borrower has no **collateral**. Banks are confident the borrower can pay back the loan. Unsecured loans usually are for smaller amounts of money, such as funds for a vacation. People who get unsecured loans likely have an account and a good relationship with the bank that is loaning the money. In most cases, these people also have a good history of repaying their loans on time.

Banks are one type of financial institution that provides loans.

Secured Borrowing

Secured borrowing happens when the lender can take away something a borrower owns if the borrower is unable to repay the loan. For example, a bank may be able to take a borrower's property, such as an office, home, restaurant, or cabin. The bank will sell this property in order to get back money that the borrower owes. In this case, the property is a form of collateral. Collateral guarantees that the lender will not lose its money if the borrower is unable to pay back the loan. Secured loans are easier to get than unsecured loans because there is less risk to the lender.

What are consolidated loans?

Consolidated loans are a type of secured borrowing. They allow a borrower to combine one or many unsecured loans into one loan. This loan is secured against the borrower's property. The advantage is that it is often easier for a borrower to keep track of making one monthly payment rather than several monthly payments. As well, the borrower often makes lower payments overall. However, consolidated loan payments are made over a longer period of time than other types of loans. The longer it takes to pay back a loan, the more interest a borrower has to pay.

What does it mean to be past due on a loan payment?

Loan payments are usually due to be paid on a certain day each month. If a person does not make the payment by that date, the payment is "past due." There may be extra fees for late payment. It may also affect the person's ability to borrow money in the future.

Why Borrow Money?

If borrowing money to pay for something costs more than paying for the item with a person's own money, why would anyone want to borrow money? The simple answer is that people do not always have enough money to buy what they want.

Imagine a person who wants to buy a new pair of jeans or a bike. It makes sense for a person to save allowance or money from jobs, such as babysitting, until he or she has enough to buy the wanted items. Sometimes, people need to make purchases that are very costly and would take a long time to save enough money to buy. For example, a car or college education costs thousands of dollars. In many places, a house costs hundreds of thousands of dollars.

People borrow money to pay for items they cannot afford to pay for immediately, such as cars, houses, and education.

Most people do not have this much money in their bank accounts. It could take years to save for these items. Borrowing money is a common way to get funds quickly.

Borrowing money can be costly, but there is still an advantage. What if a person cannot go to work because he or she cannot afford a car? That person will not have the money he or she needs to pay for food and shelter. It makes sense for the person to borrow money from a bank to buy the car. Though that person will be charged interest for borrowing money from a bank, the money will allow him or her to purchase a car. This gives the person the means to earn more money over time. In some cases, the advantage of borrowing outweighs the disadvantage of paying interest.

Borrowing money and paying it back on time helps to build good credit. Credit is the amount of money a bank or other financial institution thinks a person is capable of paying back. In other words, it is the amount of money it is willing to lend a person. A bank is unlikely to lend money to someone who either has bad credit or no credit history at all. Without good credit history, a bank has no way of knowing whether a person is likely to pay back a loan on time.

Behind the Scenes

What happens when a person or business tries to get a loan?

An individual or business applies for a loan with a bank or credit union.

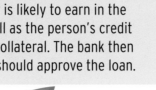

The bank looks at the amount of money the borrower is likely to earn in the future, as well as the person's credit history and collateral. The bank then decides if it should approve the loan.

If the loan is approved, the bank determines the type of loan (secured or unsecured) and payment terms (interest rate, length of payment, and fees for service).

The borrower makes regular payments with interest to the bank to repay the loan.

The borrower is able to pay back the loan. The bank makes money from the interest rates it charges and continues to lend money to other low-risk borrowers.

The borrower is not able to pay back the loan. Depending on the type of loan, the bank loses its money or takes the borrower's collateral to sell for the money.

NOT APPROVED

If the loan is not approved, the borrower may try to apply for a loan with a mortgage lending company.

The mortgage lending company looks at the credit history and collateral of the potential borrower. It then decides if it should approve the loan. Mortgage lending companies are more likely to approve a loan, but they charge much higher interest rates.

The borrower makes regular payments with interest to the mortgage lending company to repay the loan.

The borrower is able to pay back the loan. The mortgage lending company makes money from the high interest rates it charges and continues to lend money to other high-risk borrowers.

The borrower is not able to pay back the loan. The mortgage lending company takes the borrower's collateral to sell for the money.

REPOSSESSED

Interest Rates

Interest is a fee charged for borrowing money. Interest works in two ways. First, banks charge interest on money they lend. Banks take a risk when lending money. The borrower may not be able to pay back what they owe. Borrowers must pay a fee for every dollar they borrow. The money borrowed is called the **principle**.

People who borrow money over a longer period of time pay higher rates because the bank is taking a risk for a longer time. Rates also are higher for people who have had trouble paying their debts in the past. How many people want to borrow money and how much money the bank has to lend both affect the interest rate as well.

Banks pay interest to people who deposit money into a bank account. The bank borrows this money to loan to

When people borrow money, they typically pay interest on the amount they owe.

others. In the same way that a person pays a bank for borrowing money, banks pay people for using their money.

Simple interest is a **flat rate** paid on money borrowed. Assume the interest is 15 percent per year. If a person borrows $100, he or she would pay $15 in interest at the end of the year. Fifteen percent of the original amount borrowed is added each year that the money remains unpaid. After two years, that person would pay $30 in interest and $45 after three years.

Compound interest is paid on money borrowed, as well as interest and other fees. If the interest is 15 percent per year and a person borrows $100, after one year, $15 in interest

would be due. However, the next year, the person will pay 15 percent interest on the new balance of $115. The balance owing after two years is now $132.25. After three years, the person will owe $152.09.

⊞FAQ

What is the rule of 72?

Imagine a person has $10 in his or her bank account. How long would it take for that person to double his or her savings through compound interest without adding any money to the account? The rule of 72 is a formula that can be used to find out how long this will take.

72 / interest rate = number of years to double the money

Using this rule, and assuming the account has a 15 percent interest rate, the savings will double in 4.8 years.

Paying with Plastic

Today, few people pay for goods and services with cash. Plastic credit cards and **debit cards** are the most common way to pay for items. Credit and debit cards can be used in almost all stores, restaurants, and other businesses.

Credit and debit cards are easier to carry than cash, and they can be replaced if lost, stolen, or damaged. If a person loses a $20 bill, there is no way of returning it to that person if it is found. A plastic card has the cardholder's name on the front, as well as the bank's logo. If a card is lost, it can be returned to the owner.

Plastic cards are protected by security measures so that they cannot be used by people other than the owner of the card. This is to help protect people from **fraud**. For example, credit cardholders sign their name on the back of the card. When the card is used to pay for an item, the cashier checks the signature on the receipt

Clothes and meals at restaurants are examples of purchases people might charge to a credit card.

matches the one on the back of the card. When using a debit card, the cardholder must enter a **PIN**.

Credit cards allow people to buy items they want even if they do not have enough money. A bank or credit card company pays for the purchase. Cardholders receive a monthly statement showing how much they owe. They can either pay the total of their purchases or a minimum monthly payment. If they pay the total, they will not have to pay interest. However, if they pay the minimum monthly total, they will have to pay high interest rates on the remaining amount. A typical interest rate for a credit card is 18 percent. Missing a payment can damage the card user's **credit record**.

Statement of Credit Card Account

Account Number	Statement Closing Date	Current Amount Due
1876-517-908	03-15-09	$115.47

MAIL PAYMENT TO:

Jane Jones
487 Main Street
Anyplace, USA 86512-1504

FIRST BANK
51 Main Road
Anywhere, USA 96202-1542

Statement of Credit Card Account

Cardholder Name	Account Number	Statement Closing Date
JANE JONES	1876-517-908	03-15-09

Statement:	03-16-09	Payment Due Date:	04-16-09
Closing Date:	03-15-09		
Credit Limit:	$500.00	Credit Available:	$384.53
New Balance:	$115.47	Minimum Payment Due:	$10.00

Account Summary

Previous Balance:	+171.55	Transaction Fees:	+1.00
Purchases:	+27.92	Annual Fees:	+0.00
Cash Advances:	+0	Current Amount Due:	+27.92
Payment:	-85.00	Amount Past Due:	+0
Finance Charge:	+0	Amount Over Credit Line:	+0
Late Charge:	+0	NEW BALANCE:	$115.47

Reference Number	Sold	Posted	Activity Since Last Statement	Amount
32165498	03-03	03-05	Games and Beyond	$22.85
74185296	03-9	03-11	Food and Stuff	$5.07
15948265	02-12	02-14	Payment, Thank You	-$85.00
35791546	02-16	02-17	Transaction Fees	$1.00

Rate Summary

Finance Charge Summary	Purchases	Advances
Periodic Rate	18%	18%
Annual Percentage Rate	20%	20%

BORROWING VOCABULARY

FINANCE lending a customer money to buy an item; the customer makes monthly payments, including interest fees

INVESTMENT putting money into something with the expectation of making more money in return

TUITION cost of attending college or university

Big Borrowing

A car is often the first big purchase for many people. Often, a loan is needed to pay for the car. Car dealerships also will **finance** new cars.

Many people borrow money for college **tuition**. This is a good **investment** because, on average, college graduates make more money than high school graduates. Doctors, lawyers, and engineers all have a university or college education. The government gives student loans to encourage people to go to college. Students only pay interest on these loans once they graduate and are earning an income.

One of the most expensive items people buy is a house. Houses can cost hundreds of thousands dollars and take 20 to 40 years to repay. People pay a great deal of interest on home loans because of the large amount of money they borrow and the length of time they take to pay the debt.

Deciding How Much to Borrow for College

To know how big or small a student loan a person needs, he or she must try to figure out how much college will cost. This includes living expenses, assuming the person cannot live at home.

Type of expense	Estimated cost per year
School fees	$_____
Books	$_____
Internet access	$_____
Housing	$_____
Supplies	$_____
Food	$_____
Laundry	$_____
Transportation	$_____
Clothing	$_____
Health care	$_____
Entertainment	$_____
Other expenses	$_____
Total expenses	$_____ x 4 years
TOTAL	$_____

Starting a Business

Starting a business can be very expensive. In order to open a restaurant, for example, a business owner needs money to buy or construct a building complete with a kitchen, bathrooms, and dining area. The owner needs a special license to serve food and drinks. Owners also need to buy insurance against fire, floods, or other unexpected events.

Once the restaurant has opened, the owner needs money to operate the business until it turns a **profit**. Staff, such as cooks, servers, and dishwashers, need to be paid. Supplies need to be purchased, and electricity, water, and heating bills also need to be paid.

Anyone with a **marketable** idea who is willing to work hard can start a business. A person might want to consider starting a snow removal or lawn-mowing business. He or she may need to buy supplies, such as shovels and rakes.

Restaurant owners spend money on wages, supplies, and utilities.

Until a business makes money, the owner may not have the funds needed to pay for these items. The owner may need to borrow money. Friends or family may be able to provide a loan.

The owner may write up a business plan to show them why they should invest in the business and how it will make a profit. The plan would include how much the person wants to borrow and the interest rate he or she expects to pay. It would explain why the potential business owner is a good fit to run this company, provide a complete overview of the business, why the idea is marketable, and who will use the business.

⁞FAQ

What is an investor?
When people lend money to businesses, they hope to make more money. These people are investors. They use their own money to fund business projects in exchange for a percentage of the business's profits.

What are demographics?
Demographics refers to a select group of people that share certain characteristics. These groups can be used by governments and research groups to collect statistical data. For example, a group of women aged 25 to 40 or people who live in specific community are two demographics. Business owners should know which demographic their product or service is geared toward.

Bankruptcy

When people cannot pay back their debts in a reasonable amount of time, they must file for bankruptcy with the government. People who file for bankruptcy have no way to pay back the money they borrowed. Bankruptcy leads to very bad credit. After going bankrupt, it is difficult to get approval for a mortgage, a credit card, or any other type of loan.

The **consequences** of declaring bankruptcy vary from state to state. Usually, the government sells the bankrupt person's **assets**. The money made from the sale goes toward paying off the person's debts. The bankrupt person also pays a percentage of his or her **wages** to the government for a set period of time to help repay the debt.

Borrowing Careers

There are many different jobs related to borrowing. These are just two examples.

Mortgage Brokers

In return for a fee, a mortgage broker negotiates with lenders to help a person get a loan for a house. Mortgage brokers collect information needed to apply for a loan. This may include credit history, assets, **salary**, and place of employment of the person applying for the loan. Mortgage brokers decide how much to charge for their services by adding a markup, or fee, to the interest rate on a loan. Different mortgage brokers charge different markups. Despite markups, mortgage brokers can shop for the best terms and interest rates available because they deal with many lenders every day.

Each state has its own laws about the qualifications a person needs to become a mortgage broker. In almost every state, however, a mortgage broker needs a license. In some states, brokers need to attend classes. There are about 40,000 mortgage brokers in the United States.

Debt Collectors

A debt collector is someone who regularly collects debts of money. Debt collectors try to take money from people who either do not want to or cannot pay their debts. It takes an understanding and patient person to be a debt collector. Most debt collectors have some special training. The International Association of Professional Debt Arbitrators training course can be taken by a person considering a career in debt collection.

What Have You Learned?

1 What are the two basic types of loans?

2 Who invented the first credit card?

3 What are some examples of big purchases for which a person might need a loan?

4 What is "love money"?

5 How are credit cards protected from fraud?

6 What is the rule of 72?

7 What is bankruptcy?

8 What is compound interest?

9 How does a person build good credit?

10 What are two types of borrowing careers?

Answers

1. unsecured borrowing and secured borrowing

2. Frank McNamara

3. a car, college tuition, a house, or starting up a business

4. a term for money borrowed from family and friends

5. Before a shopkeeper will accept a credit card as payment, he or she will ask for a signature to prove the person using the credit card is the card's owner.

6. a mathematical formula used to find out how long it takes to double money earning compound interest; 72 / interest rate = # of years to double the money

7. when a person or business cannot pay back its debts; assets are sometimes taken away and sold to repay the debt

8. interest that is calculated on the original balance, or principle, of the funds as well as any interest that has been added to the balance

9. by repaying borrowed money on time

10. mortgage brokers and debt collectors

Spot Counterfeit Bills

Fraud is committed by people stealing money or by people who try to use fake money as real money. Sometimes, it is difficult to tell counterfeit, or fake, money from real money.

Paper money has special security features to help people tell if it is fake. Read the tips below for spotting a fake. Try to find all of the security features on a $5, $10, or $20 bill.

1. Look for fine lines in the border and on the face of president. On real bills, the lines are clear and distinct, not fuzzy.

2. Find tiny red and blue fibers throughout the paper. Fake bills often have red and blue lines drawn on them instead.

3. Hold the bill up to a light and look for the watermark. A watermark is a faint image. All U.S. bills have a watermark that matches the portrait of the president on the bill.

4. Hold the bill up to a black light. A security strip in the bill will glow. Five dollar bills glow blue, ten dollar bills glow orange, and twenty dollar bills glow green.

5. Feel the bill. Real bills are made from cotton rag rather than paper. It will feel different. The ink on a real bill is also slightly raised. You should be able to feel the texture of the ink on a real bill.

Further Research

Many books and websites provide information on borrowing. To learn more about borrowing, check out books from the library, or surf the Internet.

Most libraries have computers that connect to a database for researching information. If you input a key word, you will be provided with a list of books in the library that contain information on that topic. Nonfiction books are arranged numerically, using their call number. Fiction books are organized alphabetically by the author's last name.

Websites

Read fun facts or play games by visiting the U.S. treasury website for kids. Design your own bill by clicking on the Bureau of Engraving and Printing.

www.ustreas.gov/kids/

Create your own profile page while learning to manage your money through an online fictional spending, saving, and borrowing account.

www.fiftyp.com

Glossary

assets: items of value, such as properties, owned by a person or company

barter: to trade goods and services without the exchange of money

collateral: valuable items a person owns and can promise to give to the money lender if he or she is unable to repay debts

compound interest: interest that is calculated on the original balance, or principle, of the funds as well as any interest that has been added to the balance

consequences: results of an action

credit record: a record of a person's or company's borrowing and repayment history

currency: type of money used in a certain country

debit cards: bank cards that allow a person to automatically withdraw money from their bank account to pay for something; similar to a credit card, but the money is not borrowed

debts: money or other items that are owed

economy: the production, distribution, and consumption of goods and services

fee: money paid for a service

finance: lending a customer money to buy an item; the customer makes monthly payments, including interest fees

flat rate: a single, fixed fee for services

fraud: an illegal act when a person lies in order to steal money

global recession: worldwide economic slowdown

insured: protected against damage or loss

interest: money paid at a regular rate for the use of a loan

investment: putting money into something with the expectation of making more money in return

marketable: a product or idea that is able to be sold

Mesopotamians: ancient peoples who lived in the region of southwestern Asia that is now known as Iraq

PIN: number password that protects a credit or debit card from being used by the wrong person; every time a purchase is made, the cardholder must provide the number password

principle: the value of the money borrowed before interest

profit: money made from investing; do not include money borrowed

restrictions: limitations or rules on wh can borrow money

salary: the amount of money a person makes at his or her job in a year; not based on an hourly rate

stable: stays the same

tuition: cost of attending college or university

usury: in ancient times, defined as charging a fee or interest for the use of money; modern day definition is charging unfairly high interest rates for the use of money

wages: the amount of money a person makes at his or her job at an hourly rate

Index